Respect

Respect

The Martial Arts Code of Conduct

by Terrence Webster-Doyle

WEATHERHILL

Special thanks to our photographer, John Seberg (Seberg Photography, Inc., on the web at www.seberg.com), and to Damon and Kimber Hill and the students of the Modern Martial Arts Academy, DeLand, Florida.

First edition, 2002

Published by Weatherhill, Inc., 41 Monroe Turnpike, Trumbull, CT 06611. Protected by copyright under the terms of the International Copyright Union; all rights reserved. Except for fair use in book reviews, no part of this book may be reproduced for any reason by any means, including any method of photographic reproduction, without permission of Weatherhill, Inc. Printed in China.

07 06 05 04 03 02   9 8 7 6 5 4 3 2 1

Library of Congress Cataloging-in-Publication Data available

ISBN 0-8348-0514-6

Today at our martial arts school we are learning about Respect. Respect is the foundation of the Martial Arts Code of Conduct.

Respect means acting like a gentleman or gentlewoman. It means respecting our parents, teachers, and friends. Respect also means caring for ourselves, taking care of our bodies by keeping them healthy and clean. It means eating healthy foods and getting enough exercise and thinking healthy thoughts.

The Martial Arts Code of Conduct is a set of rules to live by. Our teachers tell us that a "code" describes a way of behaving that makes a better life for everyone. It is how we act, what we do every day that allows us to live peacefully and happily with one another.

Studying the martial arts teaches us how to stop a bully from hurting us. But it also teaches us to respect the bully because a bully is just someone who has been picked on too, someone who has been hurt and feels angry. This is a part of our Code of Conduct: to act with kindness even to those who want to hurt us.

Our teachers help us understand how other people feel and how everyone just wants to be liked. They tell us that kindness—treating people like we would like to be treated—is an important part of the Martial Arts Code of Conduct.

We need to be kind to people, especially people who are less fortunate than us. If someone is very old or sick or has a disability, it may be difficult for them to do the ordinary things that we can do. We need to be kind to all living creatures. Being kind to our pets means feeding them and making sure they are not hurt in any way.

Our teachers tell us that the Martial Arts Code of Conduct is like a map. When we travel, a map shows us how to get to where we want to go. The Martial Arts Code of Conduct gives us directions to follow as we travel on the road of life, and shows us how to get along with people we meet on the way.

Courtesy is also part of the Martial Arts Code of Conduct. Courtesy is being polite, like saying, "May I?" or "Please" when we want something and "Thank you" when someone does something for us. If a new student comes to our school it is polite to say hello and to make him or her comfortable being in a new place with new people. Courtesy is really just being nice.

The Martial Arts Code of Conduct tells us about the importance of being honest. Being honest is telling the truth, to others and to ourselves. It is also acting honestly, doing what we believe is right and not doing what we know is wrong. It means treating people fairly, as we would want to be treated.

The Martial Arts Code of Conduct tells about the importance of courage. Having courage means being brave enough to stand up for what is right. If a bully is picking on someone it will take courage to make the bully stop. We also need to be brave when we are sick or lonely or bad things are happening.

Our teachers tell us that life is full of challenges and that we need to be brave to meet them with a strong spirit. We need to have courage to live the Martial Arts Code of Conduct even when others around us are being disrespectful.

Our teachers tell us that life is a test of our character. Having character means living by the rules of the Martial Arts Code of Conduct. Having character means being strong even if we feel weak inside. Having character means treating people with kindness even if we don't feel like it.

Our teachers tell us that because we are human we will make mistakes. They tell us not to judge ourselves harshly, not to think that we are bad. They say that if we make a mistake, if we are unkind or disrespectful, we should forgive ourselves and just keep on trying. As long as we are trying we are doing the best we can.

Another important part of the Martial Arts Code of Conduct is order. Order means keeping ourselves and our lives organized. It means keeping our rooms neat by putting our things in their proper place. It means doing the jobs we are asked to do by our parents and teachers, and being on time.

In our martial arts school we create order when we line up our shoes and put away our clothes and schoolbooks in our lockers. We are taught to fold our martial arts uniforms neatly and to keep them clean. When we line up in class we are asked to stand up tall, form a straight line, and look to the front. This creates order in our group and helps us to work together as a team.

The Martial Arts Code of Conduct also teaches us about humility. Humility means not taking ourselves too seriously or thinking that we are better or more important than others. Being humble means thinking of others before ourselves.

The Martial Arts Code of Conduct teaches that wisdom is understanding what makes us afraid. Our teachers show us how fear creates conflict, like our fear of bullies. They teach us that fear is created by the way we think, which creates the way we feel. And the way we think and feel creates the way we act.

When a bully tells us that he or she is going to "get us" we become afraid all the time we are waiting for the bully to do something. Every time we think of the bully, up pops that feeling of fear. That image of the bully in our brain comes from what our teachers call "conditioning." Our teachers tell us that is the way all conflict happens, from the bully on the playground to the bully on battlefield.

Conditioning is like having a picture stuck in our brains that just will not go away. The harder we try not to think the fearful thought, not to not see the scary image, the more we think about it and see it. That thought and image keeps reminding us of something in the past that we are afraid of. It is like having a bad dream but being awake.

Our teachers show us how to sit quietly and just watch our thoughts, to let them just pass through our brains without doing anything about them, just letting them come and go. It's like watching bubbles in a glass of soda float up from the bottom of the glass to the top where they just disappear.

Sitting quietly we can see how fearful thoughts and feelings are created. We see that they are only thoughts and cannot really hurt us. When we sit and just watch them, without deciding they are bad or fearful, after a while they get less and less important. Eventually they just fade away.

At the end of each class, after we have practiced our physical martial arts, we sit in a circle and talk about the Martial Arts Code of Conduct. Our teachers ask us questions and we try to answer. They call this time "Mental Sparring." It's fun to think about these things. It exercises our brains, keeping them mentally fit just like we keep our bodies physically fit.

Our teachers say that the martial arts will help us become intelligent in our day-to-day lives and in our relationships with other people. Being intelligent means stopping to think before we act. It means thinking of what the right thing to do is when we are unsure. In class we are taught how to defeat the bully the smart way—without having to fight or to run away in fear. We learn ways to stop bullying by using our brains instead of our fists.

The Martial Arts Code of Conduct also teaches us to love. Love, our teachers tell us, means being a Martial Arts Champion for Peace. True champions are those who care for their fellow human beings, who stand up bravely for what is right, and who protect all living things from harm.

A Martial Arts Champion for Peace is a real hero, like Dr. Martin Luther King, Jr., Eleanor Roosevelt, or Caesar Chavez. They were concerned about what prevented peace, that is, what created conflict among people. Like them, Martial Arts Champions are leaders who use their knowledge and skills for peace.

We are very happy to go to a martial arts school that is for peace, one that teaches us how to get along in the world. Our parents and schoolteachers are also happy because they know that studying the martial arts together with the Martial Arts Code of Conduct will help us to be safe and develop good character.

Note to Parents

The Martial Art Code of Conduct is the foundation of all martial arts, for it emphasizes living a life of good will and peace. The Martial Arts Code of Conduct is what we call "manners" or "social skills," that behavior that promotes right relationships between people. It may seem like a contradiction to teach this within the "martial" arts, arts of self-protection. But in fact this is the very place they must be taught in order to help prevent conflict in relationships. The ultimate goal of Martial Arts for Peace™ is to stop conflict before it happens. Having these social skills reduces the chance that the student will react out of fear to a possible threatening situation such as being bullied. Combined with the confidence that comes from knowing how to protect oneself, the social skills outlined in this book, and in the leader's guide that accompanies this book, can reduce the potential for conflict. This is what the martial arts are really all about—understanding and resolving conflict peacefully. Therefore Martial Arts for Peace™ has an important role to play in the lives of young people growing up in this challenging world.

This book is for children aged 4 to 9. It is probably advisable to read this book to younger children, explaining some of the concepts. Older children can read the book themselves, asking questions of you if need be. Most important is that you both understand the difference between the often violent portrayal of martial arts in the popular media, and the true spirit and goals of martial arts practice. Moreover, if you decide that martial arts practice is right for your child, make sure you choose a school that reflects these higher goals. For help in doing this, please consult *Dr. Webster-Doyle's Martial Arts Guide for Parents.*

Want to get in touch with us? Then write, call, or e-mail.

Martial Arts for Peace Association,
P.O. Box 816, Middlebury, VT 05753
800-848-6021 / 800-966-1998
mapp8@aol.com

Want to see more of our books? Then check out our web page:

www.martialartsforpeace.com

Want to order our books? Then call or e-mail our publisher:

Weatherhill, Inc.
41 Monroe Turnpike, Trumbull CT 06611
Tel: 800-437-7840 / Fax: 800-557-5095
weatherhill@weatherhill.com

DR. TERRENCE WEBSTER-DOYLE is a martial arts sixth-degree black belt, former school teacher and administrator, Juvenile Delinquency Prevention Commission task-force member, and the co-parent of five daughters. He has written 21 internationally acclaimed, award-winning books on conflict education and the martial arts, and is co-founder and director of Martial Arts Partners for Peace.